CELEBRATING THE FAMILY NAME OF WEBB

Celebrating the Family Name of Webb

Walter the Educator

Silent King Books
a WhichHead Entertainment Imprint

Copyright © 2024 by Walter the Educator

All rights reserved. No part of this book may be reproduced in any manner whatsoever without written permission except in the case of brief quotations embodied in critical articles and reviews.

First Printing, 2024

Disclaimer

This book is a literary work; the story is not about specific persons, locations, situations, and/or circumstances unless mentioned in a historical context. Any resemblance to real persons, locations, situations, and/or circumstances is coincidental. This book is for entertainment and informational purposes only. The author and publisher offer this information without warranties expressed or implied. No matter the grounds, neither the author nor the publisher will be accountable for any losses, injuries, or other damages caused by the reader's use of this book. The use of this book acknowledges an understanding and acceptance of this disclaimer.

Celebrating the Family Name of Webb is a memory book that belongs to the Celebrating Family Name Book Series by Walter the Educator. Collect them all and more books at WaltertheEducator.com

USE THE EXTRA SPACE TO DOCUMENT YOUR FAMILY MEMORIES THROUGHOUT THE YEARS

WEBB

In the quiet night when the stars align,

Celebrating the Family Name of

Webb

There shines a name both strong and fine—

Like spider silk spun in morning light,

Webb connects the day with night.

Through mist and shadow, through time's vast span,

Webb weaves the story of woman and man.

From ancient roots to skies unknown,

Their strength is found in seeds they've sown.

For Webb is more than a name passed down,

It's the quiet hum in a bustling town.

It's the loom that weaves both joy and pain,

Creating beauty from loss and gain.

Celebrating the Family Name of

Webb

The Webb family moves with quiet grace,

Their history etched in every place.

From sunlit fields to city streets,

Their spirit rises, never retreats.

Each thread they spin, each line they trace,

Builds a future with boundless space.

Like webs that glisten with dew at dawn,

The family Webb keeps pressing on.

They build with hands both steady and sure,

Crafting a world where dreams endure.

Their wisdom flows like rivers deep,

Through every heart, through every leap.

With patience learned from days of old,

Webb's story is both brave and bold.

They honor the past with gentle hands,

Celebrating the Family Name of

Webb

While shaping the future's shifting sands.

In the dark of night or morning bright,

The name Webb shines with guiding light.

A constellation woven high,

In the fabric of the sky.

From scholars wise to those who roam,

Webb finds a way to make a home.

They gather strength from roots that run,

Deep in the earth, warmed by the sun.

ABOUT THE CREATOR

Walter the Educator is one of the pseudonyms for Walter Anderson. Formally educated in Chemistry, Business, and Education, he is an educator, an author, a diverse entrepreneur, and he is the son of a disabled war veteran. "Walter the Educator" shares his time between educating and creating. He holds interests and owns several creative projects that entertain, enlighten, enhance, and educate, hoping to inspire and motivate you. Follow, find new works, and stay up to date with Walter the Educator™

at WaltertheEducator.com

Milton Keynes UK
Ingram Content Group UK Ltd.
UKHW020937041024
449263UK00011B/572